Author: Ronald B. Raphael

Author, Dad, Athlete, Scholar, Visionary, Believer, Doer, Leader, Artist, New Yorker, Trinidadian, Entrepreneur, Analytical, Filmmaker, Academic Coach

Education: Cosmetology Business, Political Science, Film Production, Data Analytics

Illustrator: Leah Morgan

High school student, Author, Artist, Activate Actress, scholar, Big Sister, College-bound

Tips Tools Techniques

"I would like to thank everyone who has put wind in my sails."

Legacy3 Publishing

Web:

LegacyLearning3.com

RonRaphael.com

Email:

Ron@RonRaphael.com

YouTube:

LEGACYOFLEARNING@legacyoflearning5019

Copyright 2023

Contents

INTRODUCTION

The Legacy of Learning[3]

"Learning is a lifelong journey.
Why not make it part of your legacy."

My Motivation

"People will tell you what to do; rarely do
they show you how."

Most people will tell you what to do with some explanation, but rarely do they give you a detailed step-by-step demonstration and the supporting logic (the why). We're told what to do but not specifically how. Parents universally subject their children to this flawed approach in the realm of academics. Educators commit this egregious act as well. We're told to get good grades, but rarely are we shown, in detail, how. It is only when the academic results are dismal that a system of order, structure, and technique comes into play. It is difficult to course-correct at this point. It makes far better sense to lay down a system of order, structure, and techniques before a major undertaking like formal education.

1

My Academic Journey

I've always been an excellent student. My intellect was a gift from God. With it, I've been able to harness complex concepts in a relatively short time span. My other gift is an impeccable memory.

My 3rd gift is unadulterated determination. These three gifts combined kept me at the top of my class on every level. I was the pseudo-dictorian in elementary and junior high school, and I finished 5th in my high school graduating class. I did all of this without knowing my ranking until the end of the game. In essence, I was competing against myself. All went well until my first year of college. I almost flunked out. I fell below the threshold GPA needed to stay in my major. There were a few factors that contributed to my demise, but I will sum it up to these three: culture shock, workload, and visceral institutional racism. The framework for the Legacy of Learning program began here.

Take heed and succeed in spite of.

At this point, let me say this clearly. Surmounting the academic workload and adjusting to the culture is within your control; racism is not. Because of the social and racial construct of our society, there will always be racial bias. Certain segments of our society enjoy racial privilege; this is also reflected in institutions of education. Everyone else, by definition, receives the negative side of this bias. Unfortunately, it does not matter how smart you are. This bias will still exist. If you are not a member of this privileged class, you will need to be 2 times better to be recognized and 10 times better to be praised. This understanding does not come from conjecture but from lived experience. You won't find specific techniques to combat the psychological effects of culture shock and racism in this learning system. I am not inclined to do so, nor am I qualified. However, I will say this: seek out institutions of learning that reflect and value who you are. Even then, "Inspect not Expect." Parents should take every precaution to shield their children from and prepare them for the harsh inevitabilities of life. If you do detect an unfair bias in your educational experience, bring it to the attention of the administration. Challenge it. My final words on this subject are to "take heed and succeed in spite of."

Now, back to the matter at hand, which is meal most flunking out as a freshman at Cal State San Luis Obispo. At the end of my 3rd quarter at SLO, I returned to Los Angeles. I began working and eventually enrolled at Santa Monica Junior College. With an environment change and a heightened consciousness, I was able to get back on track. Unknowingly, I had already begun to develop and apply the principles of this program. I graduated from Santa Monica Junior College with a 3.5 GPA and then transferred to Long Beach State University. At Long Beach State, I was driven to prove that I was not only a good student but also an elite one. I seta goal of making the Dean's List. I needed a minimum GPA of 3.8 to accomplish this goal. This is where the pieces of the "Legacy of Learning System" began to coalesce. After a few weeks of research combined with anecdotal experience, the Legacy of Learning System was sketched out.

School got harder during my junior and senior years. There was a lot more information to consume. I had to get faster just to maintain, ever mind making the Dean's List. After implementing the" Legacy of Learning" system, I made the Dean's List 3 times. I accomplished my goal. My job was done, or was it? I graduated with a bachelor's degree in political science and a minor in business. I continued using the same system to learn everything else thereafter: film production, cosmetology, life insurance, tax preparation, etc. When my children were born, I rekindled the academic portions of the system and passed it on to them. The results are astounding. Both of my children are attending elite private high schools. My 11th-grade daughter has an overall GPA of 3.65, and my 9th-grade son has posted a 4.0 GPA every year since the 1stgrade. I've shared portions of this system with institutions and individuals. I'm using these very principles to learn the ABCs of publishing so that I can produce and distribute this book. These are my receipts to show you that the Legacy of Learning System works. I'll be your coach. Let's embark on a journey that will drastically change your outlook on learning and propel you to achieve your highest potential.

You live and you learn

Most achievements that are quantifiable and long-standing require a basis of knowledge. Becoming a competent professional in as killed discipline takes a combination of

God-given talent, hard work, aptitude, focus, and, yes, time to acquire that knowledge. Findings by a now famous researcher, Dr. K. Anders Ericsson of Florida State University, found that mastering an ultra-competitive skill takes about 10,000 hours or 10 years. There will also be a plethora of ancillary skills one would need too btain to support the larger goals one may have in life. The point is learning is a lifelong journey; there is no way around it. There are many sayings built on this premise, but the most prevalent is "YOU LIVE and YOU LEARN." My revision of this quote is, "You live and you learn, so why not be a proactive participant." It is arguable that the faster we can learn, the better our plight in life.

Learning happens automatically; it is a predisposition of life. In order to survive, a species must adapt; to adapt, it must learn. We begin learning in the womb, as a fetus, as early as 10 weeks into life. Learning is instinctive; however, it is also a skill. It can be mastered and honed.

The job of teaching a specific subject (i.e. math, English, science, etc.) is the role of a professional licensed academian. A certain type of respect is bestowed upon those who dedicate their lives to teaching and do it well. That respect is offered here and is reflected in the following statement. This course is not about mastering a particular subject; rather, it's about implementing a system and developing the skills to facilitate the learning of any subject.

Studies have shown that the greatest indicator for the level of academic achievement obtained by a person is based on the academic achievements of their parents. For this reason, I encourage you to embrace this opportunity to shift your learning paradigm for the rest of your life and for generations to come.

Why the name "Legacy of Learning3?"

The title "Legacy" originated as the name of my insurance company. I packaged my services with free talks on learning. Organizations found this bonus valuable. With the "Legacy of Learning" the theme is the same: create and pass on a fruitful legacy. There are nine other major categories outlined by the 10 Life Value System in which to leave a lasting legacy. Education is number 7 on the list.

10 LIFE VALUE SYSTEM

Dr. Spencer Holman

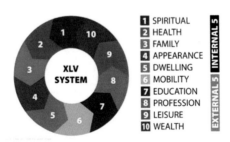

The"3" at the end of "Learning" means cubed, and it refers to the exponential learning approach.

1. You'll be told exactly what to do,
2. given a thorough explanation of why, and
3. Required to participate in interactive exercises.

Studies show that interactive learning is the fastest way to learn.

Research on Interactive learning:

Learning is more effective when active. Date: September 30, 2021

Source: Carnegie Mellon University

Summary: Engaging students through interactive activities, discussions, feedback, and AI-enhanced technologies resulted in improved academic performance compared to traditional lectures, lessons, or readings, faculty concluded after collecting research into active learning.

Ronald B. Raphael

Tips Tools Techniques

4.0 GPA CHEAT SHEET

1. Remove TV and game station
2. Keep a neat study environment
3. Register early
4. Get the syllabi for your classes early
5. Buy your books ASAP and read ahead
6. Visit an academic counselor twice a semester
7. Create a study schedule and stick to it
8. Be on time and never miss a day
9. Prepare and participate in class
10. Make 1 or 2 contacts in each class
11. Submit all work and extra credit on time
12. Adopt a healthy lifestyle
13. Get your mind and body ready
14. Use fun as a reward

Above is your 4.0 GPA cheat sheet. It is your academic achievement roadmap. Refer to it often.

1
PRE-GAME WARMUP

"Mind over matter."

The 3 pillars of this system are:

- Foundation
- Structure
- Discipline

Foundation

First and foremost is your mindset. It is your foundation. Your mindset is the ruler of all things. In other words, to raise your GPA, you have to want it to happen. It cannot be forced upon you. "What do you want?" is the foundational question. This is a great opportunity to push yourself to your academic limit with the least amount of stress. Your goal will only be achievable if your mind is set on it. What is your motivation for academic achievement? Why do you want better grades in school? The vast majority of us doit for a better financial future for ourselves and our families. After you have deliberated your answer, your first exercise begins. Answering this question will help you define your goals.

(Ex. 1: Goal Setting)

Goalsare important. Have fun, but take this exercise seriously. To aid in this goal-setting exercise, I've listed 10 categories derived entirely from the 10 Life Value System by Doctor Spencer J. Holman. If you are looking to achieve a fulfilled life, the "10 Life Value System" will help you plan a solid foundation. Write out your goals foreach category. When you get to number 7, for the sake of this exercise, be very specific. Next, you'll be populating your short- and long-term goals with the answers from the 10 Life Value System. Yourshort-termgoalsshouldspan1to2years,and your long-term goals5 to10 years. Grab a piece of paper and begin. Take as long as you need. Have fun. When you are done, print and post your long-term goals in a prominent place in your room. When I was in college, I placed mine on the inside of my narrow walk-in closet. It was there right in my face every morning while picking out what to wear for the day.

Maintaining the mindset conducive to achieving goals takes good mental and physical health. The two are positively associated butin only one direction. Mental exercise will not improve your physique. However, consistent physical exercise, a healthy diet, and rest have proven to improve our mental state. Reducing your sugar intake to the recommended fructose serving a day will increase your energy levels and restore time to your life expectancy. There is a consensus amongst medical professionals that sugar is poison. Exercise helps the body run more efficiently and is a mental stress reliever. It also helps to build discipline. We should exercise daily to some degree. Start today. It will change your life, guaranteed. Sleep is just as important as what we eat and exercise. Eight hours is recommended. Fasting once or twice a year also has tremendous healing benefits. This leads us to our next exercise.

Here is where you plan out a diet that drastically reduces salt, sugar, and processed foods. You will also be setting a daily exercise regimen. I encourage you to consult experts on these matters. I'm not a doctor.

(Ex. 2 Exercise & Nutrition)

Diet plan

Breakfast: _____

Lunch: _____

Dinner: _____

Daily Exercise plan

Goal:_____

(What, where, time, how long?)

Monday-Sunday

Sleep

Bedtime _____ pm

Wakeup time _____am

Tips Tools Techniques

Take one day a week to grocery shop and do food prep. Prep 2 or 3 meals at a time. Cook twice a week. This will save you time in the kitchen and help you maintain a consistent healthy diet by eliminating fast food. You will also save a lot of money.

My secret ingredient for mindset is accountability. Share your goals, including your plans, with someone to have them hold you accountable. The next pillar of emphasis is structure.

STRUCTURE
Environment

For the purposes of our conversation, structure and environment are synonymous. Environment includes your physical spaces, the nature of your social connections, and how you plan your life. You can have the right mindset and be subjected to a terrible environment. Yes, you can achieve your goals in a terrible environment; however, the odds of doing so will be greatly reduced.

Picture a time before TV and radio. It's almost impossible to imagine. What in the world did people do? Believe it or not, we had more social interaction and those fortunate enough to have books read for entertainment.

For this system to have its full benefit, you must convert your study environment into a place where reading is the only form of entertainment. You will do this by eliminating all forms of digital entertainment in the study space (i.e., your room). The only exception would be your personal computer, which can only be used to pursue academic objectives during study hours. This is the hardest part of the program to adjust to but the easiest to implement. Simply walk into your room and unplug the TV and game system, walk them down the hall, place them in the closet, shut the door, and walk away. Or place them in the living room. Do this now or as soon as you're able. Don't wait. This single act will be harder than cutting out sugar. The withdrawal symptoms, by comparison, will be exponentially more intense, but you will live. Welcome to adulthood, where leisure is earned and planned.

You now have an impenetrable academic sanctuary, a safe haven designed for your enlightenment. You have created a space that is dedicated to your goals, devoid of distraction. The majority, if not all, of your studying will take place here.

There is another important component: all of your studying should take place at a desk or tabletop. The bed is only for sleeping. Study inginbed makes it difficult for the mind to separate sleep time from study time. It's understood that invariably you will get tired while studying. When the need for rest arises, simply push away from the desk, walk over to your bed, lay down, and rest. In the structure of the Legacy of Learning System, sleep is prioritized and provisioned. All we're doing here is separating the 2 activities.

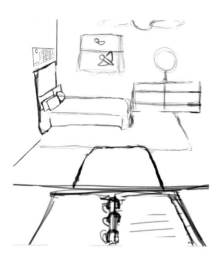

DISCIPLINE
"Beginning with the ending in mind."

Discipline is necessary to execute consistently. Do you have the philosophy of sticking to it? Especially on rainy days? I mean that figuratively and literally. Without discipline, you might as well accept a life without many noteworthy accomplishments. Unfortunately, this is something I cannot teach. Either you have it, or you don't. Having a goal, creating a plan, executing that plan, monitoring the process, enduring the inevitable setbacks, and all the unforeseen concerns that go along with it depend heavily on discipline. Discipline can be interchanged with the word focus. There is a psychological hack for maintaining discipline. It is embodied in this well-known phrase: "Begin with the end in mind."

2
TIME

"Time is of the essence."

Time is the most valuable commodity we have in life, yet we waste it constantly. In the beginning, I professed that I would help you increase your GPA by 1 point within 2 semesters and have more time for fun than you ever had. Here is where I deliver on my claim. I am a living example. In high school, I maintained a 3.5 GPA, played varsity basketball, and worked part-time. In college, Imaintaineda3.5 GPA, worked part-time, and went to cosmetology school full-time. After graduating, I worked 2 jobs, and still, to this day, I continue the same practice. How did I do it, you might ask. I did it by simply eliminating all of the distractions. Remember I instructed you to clear your room of all distractions (TV, Games, etc.). It was to recapture lost time. Removing the TV alone will save you 14 to 21 hours per week. Once this time is recaptured, an organized, prioritized system is next. This leads us to our next exercise.

(Ex.3 Time Management)

You're going to need a blank weekly calendar sheet with the hours designated (ex. 6a-10p) and a scratch piece of paper. For the blank calendar, go to the internet and print one out. If you cannot print, draw one by hand with a ruler. You will also need a rainbow set of highlighters. Now, write down everything you have to do (school, practice, workouts, work, sleep, etc.) and the time frames they occur.

Sunday	Monday	Tuesday	Wednesday	Thursday	Friday	Saturday

Everything else is unstructured time or free time. This is time wasted on a weekly basis. Most of us are wasting 14 to 30 hours weekly. We'll use this recaptured time to accelerate progress. What you'll do now is fill that unstructured time with specific activities associated with your list of goals. For students, this is the time to bring out that registration email/letter with your list of classes for the upcoming semester. Plug those classes in first. Study time is next. It is estimated that for every hour spent in class, you will need approximately 1-2 hours of study time. For a full-time student in college, you will have 4 classes with about 12 hours spent in class a week. The result would be 12-24 hours of study time a week. For high school students, the range is typically 10-20 hours of study time a week.

Study time example:

College 4 Classes = 12-24hrs/wk
High school 5 classes = 10-20hrs/wk

Lastly and most importantly, carve out time for fun as a reward. After your priorities are completed, reward yourself. Set daily, weekly, monthly, and project-ending reward categories. On a daily basis, you might reward yourself after your study time is completed with a TV show or half an hour of social media. You must set a general start and ending time. Remember, no TV or video games are permitted in your study space. Do these activities in another room. On a weekly basis, you might choose Friday or Saturday night to hang out with friends for a couple of hours. On a monthly basis, the reward might be a planned outing/event. I cannot emphasize enough the importance of implementing this reward system. These brakes help relieve stress and boost morale by compartmentalizing the overall goal into incremental achievements. Use the highlighters to color-code your calendar.

3
THE GAMES BEGIN

"Begin with the end in mind."

So, you send out applications to your schools of choice. A few months go by, and you get a letter in the mail from your number one choice that reads, "Congratulations, you have been accepted." A month later, you will receive your registration date. It's normally late spring for freshmen. After a summer of euphoria, about 3 weeks before the 1st semester, reality sets in. It's time for the games to begin. Let's focus on these phases for a moment.

The Application
"First come, first served"

We have dealt with mindset, environment, discipline and time. Now, let us move on to the game of accelerated academic achievement. It begins with the application process. Take your application process seriously, fill forms out thoroughly, attach all required documents, and apply early. Spaces are limited; first come, first served. Your acceptance or denial may hinge upon timing, not necessarily on your accomplishments. Also,

19

typically, the earlier you submit a complete application, the earlier your registration date is designated.

Registration
"The early bird gets the worm."

Soon after your acceptance letter, you will receive communications regarding your registration time and date. Place it on your calendar immediately. Missing registration dates and/or times will Make it harder for you to get your desired classes and consequently prolong your stay in school.

Before the actual day you register, it is important to do the following. Sit down with your class schedule and your college catalog, which is a book listing the classes for each degree. Referencing your degree, map out 5 options (A-E). Option (A) would represent your ideal schedule if you were indeed able to get every class at the times you desired; this is not probable. Plans (B-E) allow you to think ahead of alternative scenarios. On the day of registration, login at the time given. Choose your 4 to 5 classes based on your plan outlines. It may take 30 to 45 minutes. Once you work it all out, take a sigh of relief. You're officially enrolled!

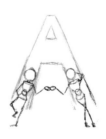

Tips Tools Techniques

Priority Registration

There are ways to get priority registration after your freshman year. I found that participation in extracurricular activities was the most effective method. For your participation in on-campus organizations (collegiate sports, student government, band, clubs, etc.), you are rewarded with an earlier registration date.

Campus & Faculty Tour

They say the best at anything makes it look easy. Somehow, what is difficult for you seems effortless for them. To them, the game has slowed down so much that they can anticipate all the upcoming moves. But what we don't see is the work that got them there. Time to put in work. Your next assignment is showing upon campus early. While most students will be showing up the week of school, I suggest that you show up for a visit soon after the faculty is back from their summer break, if you can. The faculty and staff are on campus weeks before the students are due for the upcoming semester. Take your class schedule, map out all of your classes, and visit each professor listed. This leads us to exercise 4.

(Ex. 4 Campus Mapping)

1. Print out a map of your campus or use the one inside the schedule of classes.
2. Plot out your classes for the upcoming semester.
3. Plot department head offices.
4. Plot professor offices.
5. Plot counselor locations.
6. Plot other important locations (student unions, libraries, etc.)

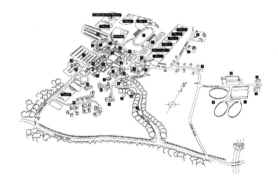

Professor Psychology
"Teachers are people too."

Understanding the psychology of each of your professors yields higher scores. Professors/Teachers are people too. They have likes, dislikes, biases, points of view, preferences, beliefs, affiliations, etc. It's your job to find the frequency at which your professor resonates and reflect that to him in your coursework. The following techniques are useful:

1. Talk to students who took the class.
2. Prep and participate.
3. Sit in the same spot.
4. Be on time and don't miss any days.
5. Communicate openly, including emails and visits during office hours.

Collect the syllabus from each professor while getting to know the compass. Use the opportunity to develop a rapport with your professor. Review the syllabus. Ask questions about the workload and what books you should or should not buy immediately. This will save you money at the bookstore and time by directing you to points of emphasis for the upcoming coursework.

In regards to an early campus visit, many institutions have implemented mandatory summer bridge programs for the very purpose of acclimating freshmen in this way. Freshmen are required to attend a 2-6 week program before the beginning of the fall semester. It includes academic classes, outings, games, and free time for social interaction. Follow the next step whether or not you participated in Summer Bridge.

Now you know what books to buy, where should you go next? Yes, the bookstore! Itis open and ready to take your money. Take all the valuable information you gathered from your professors to the bookstore. Purchase only what you were instructed. Take this opportunity while on campus to visit an academic counselor, along with other faculty staff. Shake hands, kiss babies, and have fun. You will need to call on these relationships throughout your four- year stay at school and beyond.

So, you make it home. You left a good impression on the faculty and staff. Bravo! Now that you have the book sand the syllabi in front of you weeks before the start of class, it would behoove you to take advantage of the head start, which brings us to the next exercise. A day soon after you acquire your course material, review it all.

(Ex. 5 Book/Material Review)

1. Pair each syllabus with their respective books and coursework.
2. Calendar the due dates of all assignments and tests.
3. Review each text book from cover to cover (the author, foreword, dedications, publisher, table of contents, glossary, etc.).
4. Set up a schedule to read the first 2 chapters in each assigned book in preparation for the first test and assignments.

4

THE GAME PLAN[3]

"K.I.S.S - Keep it simple, stupid"

Counselor (x2)

Congratulations! If you made it this far, you are, without a doubt, on the path towards a high-achieving semester. If you have not already, it is time to see a counselor. You will need their help to navigate the course curriculum accurately. Your course curriculum lists classes needed to graduate in a particular discipline and obtain your diploma or degree. This information is found in a massive book called The Catalog. It houses all the disciplines and all the requirements needed to achieve each of them. Your counselor will provide you with this list for your major. Keep it near and check the classes off at the end of each semester until you graduate. You'll visit two counselors each semester to ensure you're on track. The reason you use two counselors is to have them check each other for any errors. Counselors are all over campus. They're in your department, the library, the student union, etc. They're all at your disposal. This practice will ensure that you do not miss a class and, as a result, not miss your projected graduation date.

Student Grade Evaluation

1. Class Preparation and Participation
2. Assignments
3. Exams & Note-taking

By design, these three categories align with how most teachers/professors derive your cumulative grade.

Preparation and Participation

Preparation for many is the biggest problem, but if you have completed all of your exercises thus far, we've already solved it. By taking your campus faculty tour, purchasing your books and reading ahead, you have successfully prepared for the beginning of the semester. If you have not, then get on it.

Shining at class work and participation is all about preparation. Staying ahead is the key. With the Legacy pre-game semester routine, you will stay two weeks ahead of the course material. Being familiar with the major concepts of a lecture beforehand will enhance learning and facilitate participation. This sort of engagement increases your class participation score.

Assignments

There is a great feeling of accomplishment when a major task is completed. It feels better when a deadline is met. Conversely, when you don't deliver on time the feeling is quite the opposite. I suggest you get in the habit of delivering on time. You do this by planning and always starting early. Typically you would double the time the project may take and start accordingly.

Taking Exams

Here's where we completely demystify test-taking and eliminate cramming forever. This technique is called" Test-Prep." For all intents and purposes, attending school places you in a constant state of test- prep. Your mastery of the course lessons will be evaluated throughout the semester. There will be quizzes, exams, midterms, and finals as a normality. Except for the occasional pop quiz, we know exactly when they will bead ministered. Divide each class by the number of tests you'll be taking. Throughout your semester, only study material associated with the next exam is used.

Tips Tools Techniques

You eliminate cramming for any test by reviewing your Lecture notes immediately after class daily.

How you do this is key. Every time you leave a lecture, you must review your notes immediately by giving yourself a 10-minute mini- lecture. After the next lecture, do the same thing but begin from the first lecture for that test period. This technique includes speaking as if you were giving a summarized lecture in your own words to someone else. By test day, you would have reviewed this information multiple times. Instead of relearning lecture information before the test, you reinforce lecture information continuously. As a result, retention and recall goes up. Cramming will only cause stress and can indeed make you forget something you already know.

Legacy Note Taking

From the onset, most people will take notes by attempting to write a lecturer's words verbatim as he speaks. This is called dictation. The lecturer begins to speak, and we soon thereafter begin to write. Inevitably, something is missed because It is quite difficult to simultaneously listen for understanding and write. At that point, your next move is to ask the person next to you to fill in the blanks, compounding the distraction by including another.

Taking notes is a listening exercise, not a writing exercise. Before the lecture begins, place your pen on the desk. Listen for understanding. Only pick your pen up when you hear a concept that is noteworthy or highlighted by your professor. When writing the actual note, remember to condense and paraphrase. Sometimes, it is a keyword or a phrase designed to trigger a thought. A quick sketch or a pneumonic device often helps solidify a concept. Use a combination of all of the above while developing your unique style.

Tips Tools Techniques

Taking notes is a listening exercise, not a writing exercise.

The night before your exam, all you will need is a quick review of major points and a good night's rest. If you don't know it by then, it's too late.

Studies have shown that people forget immediately after an average of 50% of the lecture information presented. After 24 hours, we lose 70%-80% of new information learned. The

Legacy note taking system will help you cultivate a 60-80% memory retention rate.

5
READING AND WRITING PAPERS

"Garbage In, Garbage Out"

By far, the two areas of your course load that will cause you the most angst are the required reading and the multiple lengthy papers you will be required to write. These 2 activities will consume a sizable amount of your time. The reading will be continuous, and the writing of papers will happen in spurts. The time you saved by removing your TV and game station from your room or study area will be instrumental here.

Reading with Purpose

To surmount the enormous amount of reading required, I recommend reading daily at regimented times. Intervals are recommended; breaking up study sessions in general leads to better retention. Set a minimum number of chapters That will allow you to stay prepared for each class session. Some classes will have more reading than others, but typically, you'll be reading 1 to 2 chapters a week per class.

4 classes x 1 chapters = 4 ch/wk

4 classes x 2 chapters = 8 ch/wk
Range of 4 to 8 ch/wk.

This is not reading for entertainment or leisure; you must read with a purpose. Your goal is comprehension first and speed second. In actuality, comprehension improves speed. To gain context before you read the textbook assignments, I recommend reading the intro, the foreword, the dedications, the table of contents, and the "About the Author" section. Before you begin reading the main text, you will have gained valuable context. Context will allow you to see the landscape before you traverse it. Once you become accustomed to the style and cadence of your author, predicting his next point will become intuitive. The more you read, the easier this will get. It is called reading with foresight or "Reading Ahead." Having an idea of what's coming next facilitates maximizing speed.

To assist you in this endeavor of maximizing speed, I recommend reading the first and last sentences of each paragraph. The reason is that the first sentence is often the topic sentence, and the last sentence is often the conclusion, with a transition. If needed, you then will double back and read the chapter in its entirety. On many occasions, I found that reading the topic sentence and the concluding sentence was sufficient for overall comprehension. I call this process mental outlining. Mastering this technique will enable you to consume a vast amount of reading, with comprehension, in progressively shorter time periods.

Here are two more speed-effective tips before we move on. You should leave a textbook open on your desk when your reading session is over. An open book draws you in, and it will make it easier to begin your next reading session. Lastly, read, or study in general, for 50-70 minute intervals with a 10-15 minute break. Our minds process and store information more effectively in these intervals.

Tips Tools Techniques

Mental Out lining - Reading the 1st and last sentences of a chapter.

Steps
1. Read the About the Author, foreword, etc.
2. Set a schedule based on chapters per week.
3. Take note of the chapter length in pages.
4. Read the first and last sentences of each chapter.
5. Take notes in the book with a pencil.

6. Read in 50 to 70-minute intervals.
7. Leave a textbook open on your desk.
8. Read as if listening to the author speak.

Writing Papers

I have not met anyone who derives pleasure from writing papers for school. It is arguably the thing that students hate the most. Unfortunately, there is no easy way. However, there are techniques available that would make it less stressful.

First and for most, start as early as possible, keep ingin mind that the rule of thumb is to write a page a day. There will be 3 phases:

1. Planning/Outline
2. Research/Support
3. Writing/Recording

Planning & Outline

In the planning phase, you will determine your topic, the approach, and the tone of your paper. Examples of this would be narrative, descriptive, persuasive, expository, comparative, etc. Your professor may grant you latitude on a topic and approach, or he may be specific. Here is where you'll do your rough outline. It will contain the subject and the key areas that will be covered in your paper. The length of the outline should coincide with the intended length of the paper. Each major bullet point will represent a page roughly. For example, if you have a10-page paper, you will create an outline with 10 major bullet points. Simple enough, right?

Research & Support

Here is where you will gather all of the information needed to expand on each bullet point that supports the topic. This information may be found in the assigned textbooks and elsewhere. Take detailed notes of your sources; you will need to cite them as part of your paper to avoid plagiarism. Plagiarism is the act of taking someone else's written work and submitting it as your own. It is a serious offense.

Writing & Recording

If you have planned and researched earnestly, the writing phase will be a rudimentary task. You will employ the same-segmented approach used for reading lots of material. Write roughly a page per day, with a goal of completing it at least 3 days before the due date. You will use the remaining time for proofreading and rewrites. You will never have a paper fall short of the page requirement. I found the opposite to be true. In fact, you will have more pages written than the requirement and will be forced to cut portions out. Most professors will grade you down for falling short or going over the assigned number of pages.

When it comes to transcribing your ideas into coherent text, you have 2 options: typing or audio recording. Most of us will sit down at a computer terminal and begin typing away. Before you begin, first consider this information. Humans type at an average speed of 40-60 words per minute. But we speak at an average of 150 words per minute. One is obviously faster than the other. So, which would you prefer to do, write or record your paper? It's a no- brainer at this point, I hope. Modern technology has made this choice possible. I use Google Docs and my smartphone along with my computer terminal simultaneously at times. I'm doing so now. Check out the free YouTube tutorial for detailed clarity. (Web hyperlink www._.)

Cell Phone Audio Recording

1. Take out your completed outline, which includes your introductory sentences And the supporting bullet points.
2. Go to Google Docs on your smartphone.
3. Gather your thoughts.
4. Begin recording.

This technique is exponentially faster. You will be able to edit in real time and go back for changes later. Google Drive will store your document, making it accessible from any computer. It will also provide you with mobility. Unlike your laptop, your phone is in your pocket. Whenever you have a moment of inspiration or a bit of free time, you can record a portion of your paper. Simply pull out your outline and phone.

At this point, I would like you to take a deep breath, hold it, and then exhale. Initially, this system may appear somewhat rigorous. It requires planning and discipline. However, once mastered, it will preserve at remen do us amount of time and take you to the very edge of your academic limits. Good luck, and may God bless you in all of your endeavors.

Ronald B. Raphael

Let the "Legacy of Learning3" be the Wind in your sails.

INDEX

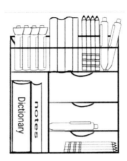

Legacy3 Publishing

Web: LegacyLearning3.com
RonRaphael.com

Email: Ron@RonRaphael.com

YouTube:
LEGACYOFLEARNING@legacyoflearning5019

Ronald B. Raphael

"I sincerely hope that this does for your Legacy what it has done for mine."

ART

GALLERY

Made in the USA
Las Vegas, NV
08 February 2024

85498269R00036